In the Forest with the Elephants

ROLAND SMITH *and*
MICHAEL J. SCHMIDT

A Gulliver Green Book
Harcourt Brace & Company
San Diego   New York   London

Requests for permission to make copies of any part of the work
should be mailed to: Permissions Department, Harcourt Brace & Company,
6277 Sea Harbor Drive, Orlando, Florida 32887-6777.

Photo Credits
Roland Smith: back cover, pages 1, 3, 7, 11, 13, 14, 15, 17, 21, 22, 24, 25, 28, 29, 33, 35, 41, 42, 46, and 54;
Michael J. Schmidt: pages 6, 8–9, 10, 18–19, 20, 32, 36, 38–39, 44–45, 48, and 56

Additional photos courtesy of Myanmar Timber Enterprise: front cover, pages
26–27, 30, 37, and 49; Khyne U Mar: pages 50, 51, 52, and 53

Gulliver Green is a registered trademark of Harcourt Brace & Company.

Library of Congress Cataloging-in-Publication Data
Smith, Roland, 1951–
In the forest with the elephants/Roland Smith and Michael J. Schmidt.
p. cm.
"A Gulliver Green Book."
Summary: Describes how elephants are trained to help in the timber camps
of Myanmar, formerly known as Burma, and their important contribution
to the selective and sustainable harvesting of teak there.
ISBN 0-15-201289-3   ISBN 0-15-201290-7 pb
1. Asiatic elephant—Burma—Juvenile literature. 2. Log transportation—Burma—Juvenile literature.
3. Draft animals—Burma—Juvenile literature. 4. Teak—Burma—Juvenile literature.
5. Loggers—Burma—Juvenile literature. [1. Asiatic elephant—Training.
2. Elephants—Training. 3. Logging—Burma. 4. Forests and forestry—Burma.]
I. Schmidt, Michael J. II. Title.
SF401.E3S6 1998
636.9′67—dc21   97-6638

B D F G E C
Printed in Singapore

Gulliver Green® books focus on various aspects of ecology and
the environment, and a portion of the proceeds from the sale of these
books is donated to protect, preserve, and restore native forests.

The text type was set in Minion.
The display type was set in Berlin Poster.
Color separations by Bright Arts, Ltd., Singapore
Printed and bound by Tien Wah Press, Singapore
This book was printed on Arctic matte paper.
Production supervision by Stanley Redfern
Designed by Lydia D'moch

This book is dedicated to the oozies of Myanmar
and their families—long may they prosper
in the forest with their elephants

—*R. S. and M. J. S.*

A Forest Partnership

A CENTURY AGO there were more than a hundred thousand elephants living in the forests of Asia. But as the needs and demands of our increasing human population have grown, most of the forests have been cut down or damaged and elephant numbers have declined sharply. Now there are only thirty-five thousand Asian elephants left and they are considered to be an endangered species.

Ten thousand Asian elephants—nearly one-third of all those remaining—live in the relatively small country of Myanmar, once known as Burma, in Southeast Asia. Though Myanmar is only about the size of Texas, five thousand wild elephants roam its forests in herds as they have for thousands of years. Five thousand more, known as timber elephants, continue to live in the forests but work there with humans to extract valuable hardwoods, including teak, which are sold around the world.

The Myanmar forest is thick with trees, vines, shrubs, orchids, and bamboo. Much of the year it is a pleasant place in which to live and work. Days are warm and sunny, and nights are cool. But during the hot, dry season, from February through April, the dust seems to hang in the air. The rivers shrink to trickles and the hardwood trees stand tall and bare. Brittle leaves crunch underfoot, and when the wind blows, the leaves rattle—sounding like rainfall.

By contrast, during the monsoon season, from May to October, it rains daily. The forest air is damp and heavy. Water drips from every leaf and vine. It flows down the steep hillsides and valleys, transforming the dry riverbeds into rushing highways for floating logs.

The Asian elephant is the only endangered species that has a working partnership with humans. In the end, this partnership may be the key to saving these elephants from extinction. It may also be the key to saving the forest where both Myanmar's wild Asian elephants and the timber elephants make their home.

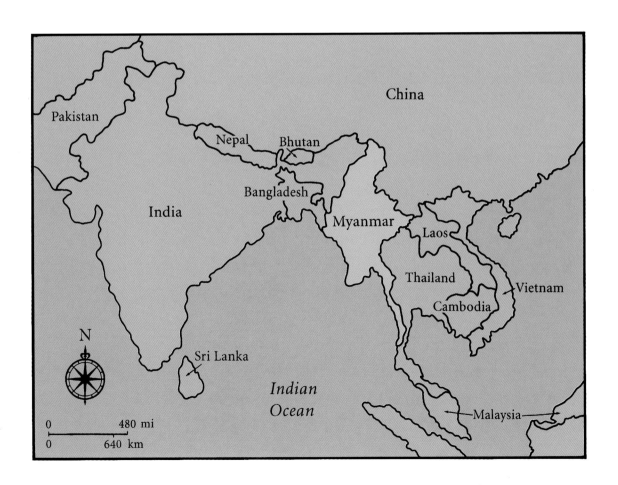

The Elephants of Myanmar

Two cow elephants have left the herd and are moving quietly away beneath the green forest canopy. The forty-year-old Win San will soon give birth to her fourth calf. She is with her best friend, Pegu.

Win San has felt the early labor pains since morning, and Pegu has been staying close to her. Pegu has given birth to three of her own calves, and she is well aware that Win San's time is near.

When cows like Pegu accompany pregnant elephants, they are called aunties. Each auntie shows great concern for her friend and will help protect the defenseless calf as soon as it is born. Elephants probably evolved this auntie system as a protection against tigers. One cow elephant alone might not be able to prevent a hungry tiger from carrying off and devouring a newborn

A timber elephant wanders through the forest.

Myanmar's vast forests are thick with trees, vines, shrubs, and bamboo.

calf. But two elephants are more than a match for even the most determined tiger.

Win San and Pegu move farther into the forest, feeding as they go. The labor pains are sharper now and Win San becomes restless. Her belly contracts as the calf within her moves into position for delivery. The contractions continue. Finally a small bulge appears beneath her tail; the calf is in the birth canal. During the next half hour the contractions intensify. Win San is very active. She lies down and gets back up again several times, trying to ease her discomfort. The bulge beneath her tail is large now. Win San bellows. With a final belly-tightening push, the big bulge moves down the birth canal and the calf is born, falling with a splash onto the forest floor.

Pegu touches the baby with her trunk as Win San turns around. Both cows sniff and gently prod the calf as it struggles to get up. It's a male weighing more than 250 pounds.

The calving took about an hour, and in less than half that time, the

calf is standing. He's three feet tall, just tall enough to reach up beneath his mother and find a teat for nursing. He will feed every two hours on her rich milk, drinking one or two quarts at a time, gaining a pound per day.

If Win San and Pegu were wild elephants, the two cows would rejoin the wild herd in a day or so. But they are timber elephants. . . .

THE MEN WHO RIDE the timber elephants in Myanmar are called *oozie*s. Maung Mint, Win San's oozie, sits inside his hut with a group of other oozies and rolls the dice. Nine! He wins again. As the others grumble at Maung Mint's round of good luck, he gathers up his winnings.

"We've been playing all night and the sun is rising," Maung Mint says. "I'm finished with the dice."

"But it's our day off!"

"Still," he says, "I need to check on Win San. I have a hunch that she's had her calf."

The other oozies laugh. "A fool's errand!" one says. "Who can tell when a cow will calve?"

"All the same," Maung Mint replies, and waves good-bye to his fellow oozies.

He'd been expecting Win San to calve any day now. When he set her free in the forest yesterday afternoon, she seemed a bit uneasy. Her friend Pegu was staying close by her, which convinced Maung Mint that the birth was near.

Maung Mint finds Win San's tracks and follows them. As the path leads him deeper into the forest, he becomes more sure that his hunch is correct. He knows that elephants always find a secluded place in which to give birth.

It takes him more than two hours to find the elephants—all three of them! Maung Mint is pleased. The newborn calf is up and nursing.

A timber elephant camp

Friendships between oozies and elephants begin at an early age.

The cows rumble in alarm and turn to face him with a surprising quickness. He speaks to them soothingly, and they settle down when they see it is an oozie, not a tiger.

Maung Mint walks up to Win San. As he gives her a friendly pat, her calf comes right up to him and pulls on Maung Mint's arm with his stumpy little trunk.

Maung Mint laughs. "You're a bold one!"

He takes a good look at the calf. The little bull is well formed and active. He'll make a fine addition to the timber camp.

After about an hour, Maung Mint starts back to camp to get his young grandson, Won Lin. He had promised Won Lin that he would show him the calf as soon as it was born.

Back in the village, Maung Mint tells his family the exciting news. He barely has time to gulp down a cup of tea before his grandson tugs him back into the forest.

When they reach the elephants, Won Lin is amazed by the miniature calf. "What will you call it?" the boy asks his grandfather.

Maung Mint thinks of the game the night before. "I'll call him Toe Lai," he says. "Dice game."

"Can I be Toe Lai's oozie, Grandfather?"

"If you study hard and become skillful, you may well be Toe Lai's oozie one day," Maung Mint replies.

IN MYANMAR half of the timber elephant population is owned by Myanmar Timber Enterprise (MTE), which is operated by the Myanmar government. The other half is owned privately, and those elephants work in the forests under contract to MTE.

In the past elephants became timber workers in one of two ways: They were either captured in the wild, or they were born to a timber elephant cow in a logging camp. Because their numbers have declined in recent years, few elephants are taken from the wild. Instead of catching wild elephants, MTE managers are working on better ways to breed their own replacement timber elephants.

By the time it is six months old, a calf born in a logging camp is given an identification number, which is sometimes tattooed on its rump. When the number is assigned, a record book is started. The book will follow the elephant wherever it goes, and every significant event in the elephant's life, from its birth to its death, will be recorded.

Until it is four or five years old, the baby elephant remains with its mother, even while she works in the forest dragging heavy logs. This stage of life is called Calf at Heel. During this time no active training is done, but the calf still learns many things.

Baby elephants are intelligent, curious, and mischievous. Like human children, they spend many years learning what it takes to become an adult member of their society. One way a baby elephant learns is by observing and copying what its mother does.

Calves also learn by playing with other young elephants. They wrestle and chase one another, learning how to assert themselves and gain status within the herd.

LEFT: *Notes are made in a timber elephant's record book by the elephant's oozie and by veterinarians who care for the elephant through the years.*
BELOW: *A two-year-old calf follows its mother.*

At the age of four or five, the calf is separated from its mother. A five-year-old elephant weighs at least a thousand pounds—as much as an adult horse. It is old enough and large enough to begin its training to become a timber elephant.

Young elephants do not know their own strength. So for the first few weeks of training, they are securely tied into a log chute called a crush. This prevents the young elephants from injuring themselves or their trainers. The oozies stay with the youngsters around the clock during this period. They even sing to them to keep them company. After a few days in the chute, the young elephants settle down and begin to learn.

Settling down in a chute

Food is used to reward timber elephants during training.

As soon as a young elephant accepts its trainers, it's taken down to the river for a bath. This is done by enlisting the aid of special elephants called *koongyi*s (koon-gees). The young elephant is tied to one or two of these gentle but firm *koongyi*s. If it tries to resist or break away, the *koongyi* corrects the calf. It's the *koongyi*'s job to let the young elephant know that it must obey the rules. Very few elephants become *koongyi*s, as it takes a rare mix of tolerance and intelligence. The *koongyi*s are highly valued for these special qualities.

The lessons proceed rapidly, and the young elephant soon learns the commands to lift its feet and to accept an oozie sitting on its back. Like children, elephants learn at different rates. The training is adapted to suit the learning pace of each calf. After three or four weeks, most calves have a young oozie assigned to work with them and have learned the following basic commands:

Hmit (mitt) or *Mek* (mek): Lie down on your belly.

Lutt (lut): Stand up.

La (lah): Come here.

Haw (haw, how): Stay still and be calm.

Yah (yah): Stay calm and don't move your: ear, leg, foot, trunk, tail, head, and so on.

Ait (ate): Lie down on your side; sleep.

Hlay (hlay): Rest on your side.

Myaunt (myawn): Pick up your front leg so that I may use it as a step to get up on your back.

Yat (yot): Stop.

Tet (tet): Go forward, or go away.

Kaut (cowt): Pick up that object and lift it up to me.

Teh htu (teh too): Put your leg(s) into that fetter.

When its initial training is completed, the young elephant becomes a baggage elephant. It will remain a baggage elephant until it is large enough to do timber work, usually at about age eighteen.

Baggage elephants are usually kept tethered in special areas outside the oozies' permanent rest camps. Unlike trained timber elephants, they haven't yet learned to stay near camp. They are only set free in the forests when their oozies are present to keep an eye on them.

The baggage elephant's job is to carry light loads of supplies from the

This elephant knows what to do when his oozie calls out, "Ma! Ma!"

permanent rest camps to the timber elephant units working in the deep forests. They are also used during the monsoon season to bring supplies from town when the roads are impassable to other transport.

When the baggage elephant reaches the age of fifteen, it is sent to a logging camp with the timber elephants to complete its training. At the camp the elephant practices by moving lightweight logs. Doing this light work builds up the muscles it will need to become a full-fledged timber elephant.

Timber work is complicated, and the elephant must learn many new commands. Among these are:

> *Ton* (tone): Push that log (or rock, or elephant) forward.
> *Aung* (ong): Roll the log with your tusk or trunk.
> *Yon* (yawn) or *Swell* (swail): Pull the log.
> *Ma* (mah): Pick up the log on your tusks.

Two first-class timber elephants stack logs in a riverbed.

Pwint (pwint): Lift the log with your trunk.

Phel (fail): Push those branches out of the way.

When the elephant has learned all of the commands, it is ready to become a timber elephant. The elephant knows what to do and when to do it, sometimes even before the oozie asks. Man and elephant work smoothly together as a team, moving logs without wasted effort.

When the elephant is eighteen, a veterinarian examines it and decides whether it's fit enough to become a full-time timber elephant. At this stage a fit elephant is capable of pulling logs weighing one ton or less. Such elephants are known as third-class timber elephants.

Over a period of years, as the elephant becomes stronger, it can move up in class. A second-class elephant is capable of pulling logs weighing up to two tons. A first-class ranking is reserved for large bull elephants that can pull logs weighing more than two tons, or four thousand pounds. An average-size Asian elephant weighs about seven thousand pounds and stands about eight feet tall. A very large bull weighs as much as fifteen thousand pounds and stands up to ten feet tall.

Between the ages of twenty-five and forty-five, the timber elephant is at peak physical condition. After age forty-five, the timber elephant begins to decline physically. Because of this, the elephant is usually put into light baggage service until it is retired or dies of old age.

The Oozies of Myanmar

I t's dawn, deep in the Myanmar forest, and Won Lin is awake. Just as he and his grandfather had hoped, he has become an oozie. He rolls up his sleeping mat, buttons his shirt, knots his colorful *longyi* (lone-jee) around his waist, and steps into his rubber thongs.

He joins the other oozies near the warmth of the hardwood fire. They wait for the water to boil so that they can prepare green tea, which they drink from bamboo cups.

Their leader, the *singoung* (sing-ong), brings over an aluminum pot, and they share a simple breakfast of rice, curry, and vegetables left over from the night before. As they eat, they joke with each other and discuss the day's work.

After breakfast each oozie straps on a long, heavy knife, or *dah*, and sets out into the forest to find his elephant. Oozies use the broad-bladed

*Oozies carve elephant bells
with their dahs.*

An outdoor kitchen

dah to cut away branches and creepers while they are on their elephants' backs. They also use the *dah* to carve elephant bells, cut bamboo to build huts, and at times, to control dangerous elephants.

WON LIN HEADS for the shallow river near their camp. He looks up at the sky; the monsoon season will start soon. Weeks of steady rains will swell this calm river into a roaring torrent. Before then tons of timber must be moved to the riverbed so that it will be ready to be carried downstream.

As he wades across the river, Won Lin spots an iridescent blue kingfisher swooping down and spearing a small fish for breakfast. In the distance he hears the alarmed grunt of a sambar deer. Perhaps the deer has scented a leopard? The night before, Won Lin and the other oozies heard the rasping call of a leopard not far from camp.

Won Lin climbs up through the brush on the opposite bank and begins looking for the tracks of his timber elephant, Toe Lai. Toe Lai is now thirty years old. He and Won Lin have been partners for more than twenty years.

Won Lin knows the shape and size of Toe Lai's footprints, and it takes only a moment to find his elephant's trail. Along the trail, Won Lin finds a massive imprint in the wet grass where Toe Lai lay down to rest for a while. Farther down the trail he finds a lush stand of spiky bamboo, which Toe Lai ripped into and ate. By looking at these signs, Won Lin knows how Toe Lai has spent his night in the forest.

After following the meandering trail for three miles, Won Lin hears the faint but distinct sound of Toe Lai's bell. All timber elephants wear large wooden bells around their necks. Oozies carve the bells out of teak and fasten wooden clappers on the bell's sides. Each bell has a unique sound, which an oozie can pick out from half a mile away. To oozies the bells sound like forest birds, which they believe is soothing to their elephants.

A few minutes later Won Lin sees his giant gray partner. The tusker is below him on a hillside, pulling up clumps of grass. Won Lin watches as Toe Lai shakes the excess dirt off the tangled roots, then delicately stuffs the grass into his mouth.

Standing quietly Won Lin takes a moment to enjoy the view. The misty forest surrounding them is filled with thick stands of rustling bamboo. There are also *bambwe*, *nabe*, *tama*, and *tyaw* trees. And dozens of century-old hardwood trees with names like *padauk*, *pyingado*, *kudee*, and teak.

After a few minutes he calls his elephant. *"La! La! La!"*

Toe Lai fans out his big ears and looks up the hill toward his oozie. He pulls up another clump of grass and puts it into his mouth.

Unhooking Toe Lai's fetters

"*La! La! La!*"

Somewhat reluctantly Toe Lai leaves his patch of grass and makes his way up the steep hill toward Won Lin. It's time to go to work in the forest.

When Toe Lai reaches him, Won Lin squats and unhooks the chain fetters wrapped around both of Toe Lai's front legs. Timber elephants are hobbled like this so they won't wander too far from camp. Despite the fetters, some elephants manage to travel as far as ten miles before the night is over. Won Lin is pleased that Toe Lai was only three miles away this morning.

With the fetter off one ankle, Won Lin throws the extra chain over the top of Toe Lai's back.

"*Hmit!*" Won Lin commands while touching Toe Lai as far up on his back as he can reach. The bull slowly lowers himself to his belly and

Climbing up on Toe Lai's back

Oozies wash their elephants.

stretches out on the ground. Won Lin cuts a leafy branch off a nearby bush and uses it to sweep away the dirt on Toe Lai's neck and head.

"You are a very dirty elephant," he tells Toe Lai. Toe Lai responds with some deep chirping sounds, and Won Lin pats him on the shoulder.

Using Toe Lai's outstretched front leg as a step, Won Lin climbs up onto his elephant's head and sits with one foot behind each warm, leathery ear.

"*Lutt!*" he says.

Toe Lai gets to his feet and Won Lin prods him behind the ears with

his toes. Toe Lai heads back toward camp. Before they reach camp, Won Lin and Toe Lai stop at a pool in the river. A few of the other oozies have already found their elephants and are vigorously scrubbing them down.

Won Lin guides Toe Lai into the pool. "*Hmit!*" he commands, and the big elephant lies down. Won Lin stands on Toe Lai's back and hitches his *longyi* up so that it won't get wet while he works. He then steps down into the river and begins scooping up water and splashing it onto his elephant. Timber elephants are bathed every morning. To prevent

An oozie scrubs his elephant with a suyit *vine.*

chafing, the gritty dirt must be washed off the elephant's skin before the oozie puts on the dragging gear.

Toe Lai's slate gray skin glistens in the early morning sun as Won Lin scrubs him. Won Lin uses soap made from the crushed fiber of the *suyit* vine. To clean Toe Lai's white ivory tusks, he uses river sand. When every inch of Toe Lai's hide is clean, Won Lin climbs back up on his elephant's head.

"*Lutt!*" he commands. Toe Lai surges up out of the water and they head toward camp.

Won Lin stops his elephant just outside the camp near the rack where the dragging gear hangs. He pulls down several mats of soft padding called *thay-ay* and lays it on Toe Lai's back. The padding is made from the bark of the *bambwe* tree. Next comes the saddle, or *ohn-done*, which he puts on top of the padding. Over the top of this and running under the elephant's chest, Won Lin straps on the girth band, or *gok-se-gyo*. He then secures the crupper rope beneath Toe Lai's tail. The girth band and crupper rope hold the saddle in place.

Won Lin then ties the breast band, or *laibat*, across the front of Toe Lai's chest. The breast band has loops woven on either end that hold the drag chains, or *ye-laung*, used to pull the heavy timber along the ground. Finally, to prevent chafing, Won Lin daubs a generous portion of lard underneath the girth and breast bands. Now the oozie and the elephant are ready to work.

Saddled in dragging gear and ready to go to work

THE BASIC ELEPHANT working unit is made up of six elephants and six oozies. Each unit also has three assistants called *pejeik*s (pea-jakes) and three laborers to assist the oozies. The *pejeik*s' and laborers' jobs are to limb trees, cut holes in the logs for the drag chains, and attach the chains to the logs. Each working unit is supervised by a *singoung* and an assistant *singoung*.

The working season lasts eight months—from June to the middle of February. During this time the oozies leave the semipermanent rest

Two first-class tuskers and a smaller cow are ready to head into the forest.

camps, where their families live year-round, and take their elephants deep into the forests. They set up temporary camps, living in rough bamboo shelters. During the working season, they don't see their families for weeks, or sometimes months, at a time.

During Myanmar's dry season, from mid-February through April, it's simply too hot for the elephants and oozies to work in the forests. Instead they return with their elephants to the rest camps.

Oozies and their families live simple but hard lives deep in the forests. Their jungle homes are built on stilts. The walls are made of bamboo poles and woven mats. The roofs are thatched with palm leaves. They cook their meals of rice, curry, and vegetables over charcoal fires. There is no indoor plumbing, and they wash their clothes and bathe in the river.

Both men and women wear *longyi*s, tubes of colorful cotton cloth knotted at the waist. This simple dress has many advantages: It's cool during the heat of the day; it can be washed and dried in a matter of minutes; and it's inexpensive.

Oozies make a thousand *kyat*s (chots) a month. This is equivalent to about ten dollars. In addition to paying this basic wage, the government provides each oozie and his family with a monthly ration of rice.

The oozies and their families make use of the forest for such things as food and building materials. What they can't find in the forest they raise themselves. In season they plant gardens for fresh vegetables. Many families keep pigs or chickens. Pigs wander around the village freely, taking refuge underneath the huts when it gets too hot. Chickens scratch and peck around the village during the day and roost in the forest at night.

There are some items the forest doesn't provide, such as cloth, rubber thongs, and mosquito netting. For these things the oozies and their families have to go to the nearest town, which sometimes involves a round-trip of more than a hundred miles. There are no cars in the

A pregnant elephant with her oozie

timber camp. To get to town the oozies hitch rides on logging trucks or ox carts, ride bicycles, or simply walk. During the monsoon season the dusty roads turn into mud, and sometimes the only way to the nearest town is by elephant.

Living in the forest presents other challenges to the oozie and his family. Venomous snakes and biting insects are always a concern. Relentless rain pelts the village in the monsoon season. During the dry season, the fierce intensity of the sun can cause heatstroke. And if an oozie or one of the members of his family becomes ill, medicine and doctors are many hours away.

Despite the difficulties and challenges of forest living, most oozies wouldn't trade lives with anyone. They love being in the forest with their elephants.

Sometimes women and children wear a paste made from wood to protect their skin as they work in the tropical sun.

WOMEN SOMETIMES help their oozie husbands with the feeding and care of the elephants, but in Myanmar only males are allowed to become oozies.

At an early age boys begin following their fathers into the forest to retrieve their elephants. By the time they are eight or nine, these boys know most of the basic commands oozies use and how to tie fetters around an elephant's ankles.

When their fathers are away from the village working in the forest, young boys spend as much time as possible watching older boys working the baggage elephants. The oozie's skill with elephants is passed down from generation to generation.

By the time an oozie's son is twelve years old, there's a good chance that he has become a wage-earning oozie himself. The *singoung* matches the boy with a young baggage elephant, and they train together for several years before going into the forest to work. It's not unusual for an oozie to spend his entire working life with the same elephant.

Oozies can retire at half-pay when they are sixty years old. A retired oozie stays in the rest camp during the working season. He spends his time playing with his grandchildren and visiting the baggage elephant camp, where he teaches young oozies the art of working with elephants.

This young elephant and boy will work together for a lifetime.

In the Forest with the Elephants

At noon Won Lin guides Toe Lai up to the harness rack and takes off the dragging gear. In six hours they have moved two large teak logs to the river—a good day's work. After the gear is hung up, Won Lin rides Toe Lai a mile into the forest and fetters his front legs.

"You'll be able to fill your belly from here," he tells Toe Lai. "I'll see you tomorrow morning. Don't wander too far away."

When Won Lin returns to camp, the *singoung* gives him his next day's assignment.

"Won Lin," the *singoung* says, "tomorrow you and Toe Lai will start dragging that monster of a teak on the north hillside. They cut it down this morning and sectioned it into four logs."

Won Lin knows the tree well and he's not surprised that it has been assigned to Toe Lai. His elephant is a first-class elephant, capable of

Two tuskers pulling side by side

pulling more than four thousand pounds. Toe Lai is also a *koongyi*, the most intelligent and reliable elephant in the timber unit.

"I'd better take a look," Won Lin says.

The two-hundred-year-old teak is on a steep hillside near a dangerous cliff. It was selected for harvesting three years earlier. At that time the forest manager and his helpers girdled the tree. They cut away a strip of bark all around the thick trunk. Without its bark the tree died, and the hardwood has been drying since that day. The wood from this tree is destined for the deck of a large ocean liner being built in Hong Kong. Won Lin doesn't know this though. He only knows that he and Toe Lai have to get the logs from this huge tree away from the cliff, down the steep slope, then to the river two miles away.

Won Lin arrives at the spot and clambers through the thick underbrush, up the steep hillside, to the fallen tree. The four teak logs are perilously close to the edge of the cliff. He guesses that each section weighs well over three thousand pounds. If he isn't careful when he

Pa Ka Toe (Mr. Tall) drags a log to the river, where a pejeik *will unhook him.*

begins the drag, he'll lose a log over the cliff. Worse yet, a shifting log could drag both him and Toe Lai over the edge.

Won Lin walks around each log, calculating the best way to start the pull. With this information he determines which log should be hauled first. His final task is to pick the best drag path away from the cliff to the river. By the time he finishes it's getting dark. He walks back to camp, listening to the distant hollow *tok-tok-tok* of elephant bells in the forest.

Later that evening as Won Lin lies on his sleeping mat, he thinks about the next day's work. He recalls all the tricks his father and grandfather taught him about moving such difficult logs. He and Toe Lai have handled big logs in tough spots many times before, but these four logs will be especially tricky because of the cliff. He hopes Toe Lai is resting well. His elephant will need all his strength for the dangerous work ahead.

NEARLY HALF OF MYANMAR is still forested. This cover is by far the densest in Southeast Asia. One reason Myanmar's forests are still vast

and green is that much of the logging is done by elephants. Another reason is that foresters use a system of harvesting trees called the selective tender system.

Only teak trees that are at least eighty to a hundred years old are chosen for cutting in Myanmar. Before a tree is harvested, it must be at least seven and a half feet around at the height of a man's chest. In a thirty-acre area, the Myanmar Timber Enterprise (MTE) might cut down just one mature tree every ten years. To assure there will be teak trees for future generations, foresters replant thirty thousand acres of teak every year. The selective tender system has been used in Myanmar since 1856.

Before a teak tree is cut down, it is first girdled and left to stand for three years. This is so the wood can dry out, which makes it lighter for transport. After a tree is cut down, its limbs are trimmed away. Depending on its size, it is cut into three or four logs. It's now up to the *pejeik* to get the logs ready for dragging. The first thing he does is to round off the lead end of the log. This is called snouting. This makes it easier for the elephant to drag the log along the ground. With the log snouted, he then chops a hole called a *nepha*, or "earhole," in one end of the log.

The elephant's work is called stumping or extraction. This means moving the log from the stump to the collection point. The collection point is either a riverbed, where logs can be "rafted" to a sawmill, or the nearest road, where logs can be loaded on trucks.

Not all timber elephants are required to do the same amount of work. As they work, the oozie keeps in mind each elephant's class and conditioning, the weight of the logs being pulled, the difficulty of the terrain, and the season. They let their elephants rest as needed.

Still, timber elephants work hard, and during the eight-month working season, they tend to lose weight—sometimes as much as a thousand pounds. To preserve the elephants' strength, the oozies usually end the workday by eleven A.M. The elephants get three-day weekends and

LEFT: *A* pejeik *runs dragging chains through the "earhole" at the end of a log.*
BELOW: *It takes both strength and agility to stack logs.*

A first-class elephant can move logs weighing more than four thousand pounds

several one-day "holidays" each month. They also get a long "vacation," which allows them to fully recover after the strenuous working season.

The fact that elephants don't need roads to get to the trees is good for the environment. Without roads, few people can get into the forests to damage them. This keeps people who practice shifting, or slash-and-burn cultivation, from burning the forests.

The modern mechanical substitutes for elephants are called log skidders. These machines move on heavy steel tracks, causing tremendous damage to the forest. The petroleum fumes these machines spew pollute the air.

Logging by elephants is better for the environment. Their feet don't destroy the forest and they use "green" fuel, which doesn't pollute the air.

THE NEXT DAY Won Lin and Toe Lai make their way carefully up the narrow, twisting path that leads to the fallen teak. Other oozies follow behind on two good-size tuskers. When the group arrives, Won Lin guides Toe Lai to the edge of the cliff. He feels Toe Lai tighten up beneath him.

"Watch out, old fellow," he says. "We don't want to end up down there today."

The first log Won Lin wants to move is the smallest and farthest up the slope. He tells the other oozies that their elephants will need to brace the log to prevent it from rolling while the *pejeik* gets the chain set. The two oozies move their elephants into position. They give the command and their elephants bend forward, holding the log in place with the base of their trunks and the tips of their tusks.

With the log securely braced, the *pejeik* runs Toe Lai's drag chain through the *nepha* hole in the teak log. The log is ready to be pulled.

Won Lin knows they must drag the log at just the right pace. If Toe Lai pulls it too slowly, the log might roll downhill; too fast, and the log might slide straight down into Toe Lai's rear legs. Once they get past the sloped area, they'll be safe.

Won Lin gives Toe Lai a little pep talk before beginning, then shouts, "*Yon!*"

Toe Lai bellows as the chain pulls tight. The *koongyi* elephant knows there is danger for him in this place. He has been dragged backward more than once by a runaway log on a steep slope.

"*Yon!*"

Toe Lai pulls and strains, slipping to his knees under the heavy burden.

Because elephants are subject to heat stroke, heavy pulling is done in the morning, before it gets too hot.

The log shifts downward slightly, but the two tuskers keep it steady. When Toe Lai feels the log begin to move, he leans into his breast band, doubling his effort. As the log picks up speed, the strain lessens.

"*Yon!*" Won Lin shouts. "*Yon!*"

Toe Lai lunges ahead.

Won Lin, the *pejeik*, and the other oozies watch the log for the first hint of sideways rolling, but there is none. Within a few minutes Toe Lai

*When this log lands in the riverbed,
the day's work will be done.*

has dragged the heavy log out of immediate danger and reaches the top of the slope. All smiles, Won Lin and the *pejeik* congratulate each other and give Toe Lai a well-earned rest.

When Toe Lai's breathing returns to normal, they continue the drag. They make slow but steady progress moving down the steep, twisting path toward the riverbed. At each switchback they have to unhook the drag chains and reposition the massive log. The two other elephants help hold the log in place while Toe Lai's chains are reattached.

When they get close to the river, they unhook Toe Lai from the log and let him push it over the edge of a steep bank. The log crashes into the riverbed and lands nose first in the soft sand.

It's noon and their workday is done. Back at camp the three elephants are each fed a bucket of paddy rice, then taken into the forest and set free.

Tomorrow they will pull the second log to the riverbed. And the next day, another. There the logs will lie until the monsoon rains come.

Partnership and Conflict

The *singoung* hands Won Lin an urgent message from the MTE headquarters:

TAKE YOUR *KOONGYI*, TOE LAI, TO MABALA VILLAGE IMMEDIATELY. ASSIST IN THE CAPTURE OF SIX WILD ELEPHANTS.

"The village of Mabala is over a hundred miles away," Won Lin comments.

"I know," the *singoung* says. "A truck is waiting for you and Toe Lai at the Bago-Yoma road. If you leave early tomorrow morning, you'll get there by noon and be at Mabala in three days or so."

That evening Won Lin finds out more about the elephants he and Toe Lai are supposed to help capture. About a month earlier, a wild elephant herd had shown up outside Mabala.

*Elephants travel easily through
the forest, without bridges or roads.*

A wild herd moves through the forest.

They raided the villagers' rice and vegetable crops. Having enjoyed the feast, they kept coming back for more.

The loss of the precious food was serious enough, but one night when a man and his son tried to drive the elephants away, the excited elephants turned on them and chased them all the way back into their hut. Then, instead of stopping, the elephants tore the hut apart and trampled the man and boy. When informed of this tragedy, the government made the decision to capture the marauding elephants.

Three and a half days after receiving the message, Won Lin and Toe Lai arrive at Mabala. Two other oozies and their big bull elephants have also been recruited from the forest to assist in the capture.

That night when the small elephant herd arrives to feed on the villagers' crops, they are met with a surprise. Before they sense that anything is wrong, firecrackers erupt in the darkness and they are confronted by shouting people carrying torches.

The wild elephants turn in panic and run from the fire and noise. As they flee, more fires are lit on both sides of them and the awful ruckus intensifies.

To the east all is dark and calm, and that's where the elephants seek refuge. After two miles of swift flight, they sense the thick tree trunks closing in on them from both sides. Directly in their path is a gap in the narrowing walls. The lead elephant, an old cow, runs right through it. Immediately the gap closes and she is trapped.

This method of catching wild elephants has been used many times before. The marauding elephants are driven by shouting men and fire to a funnel made out of logs. When the elephants are in the trap, a heavy gate slams shut behind them.

This capture method does not always work, but this night it succeeds very well. The entire herd of six elephants is trapped inside the solid stockade of lashed tree trunks called a *keddah*.

Oozies check the outside of the keddah *wall to be sure it can hold the elephants.*

The *keddah* is eight feet high and nearly a mile around. The wild elephants make several attempts to smash their way out, but they are met by shouting men with orange-flamed torches and they lose their nerve.

During the next two weeks, Won Lin and the other two oozies skillfully use their *koongyi* elephants to catch four of the six wild elephants. They ride into the stockade with extra men on the *koongyis'* backs and slip loops of thick rope around the wild elephants' legs and their necks. Two *koongyis* wedge each captured elephant between them, pushing and dragging the animal out of the stockade. These elephants will be trained, and eventually they will become timber elephants.

The last two elephants, the old cow and her two-year-old calf, are

The wild calf is safely tethered next to a koongyi.

This wild elephant will be moved to a forest where there are fewer people nearby.

given a powerful drug by a veterinarian. He shoots the drug into them with a dart rifle from a safe distance. When the two elephants are sedated, they are dragged and pushed by Toe Lai and the other *koongyi*s into a large truck.

The next morning both elephants are taken to a forest fifty miles away and released. They'll soon find other wild elephants and join a new herd.

WON LIN AND TOE LAI stay at Mabala for several weeks to help train the wild elephants.

At night Toe Lai is tied to a tree. The forest near the village has been cut down and there is no place for him to forage. Instead Won Lin has to bring food to him. Toe Lai's weight has dropped during their stay at the village. Won Lin is concerned.

The monsoon season is well underway, and food for Toe Lai becomes even more difficult to gather. The rains are swelling the rivers now.

Heading home

This means Won Lin's elephant unit has to work twice as hard to take advantage of the flow. Won Lin is eager to get back to the logging camp to help his friends.

Finally Won Lin is given permission to leave Mabala and return to the forest. The trip back is difficult. The rains have turned the dusty roads into quagmires. Toe Lai is off-loaded a half dozen times to push or pull the truck they are traveling in out of the mud. It takes them a week to get to the Bago-Yoma road. They arrive in the evening and it's too late to head into the forest.

Won Lin ties Toe Lai to a tree and gathers food for him to eat. The cold rain hammers them without letting up. Won Lin builds a small fire and huddles near it.

"Tomorrow," he tells Toe Lai, "you'll be in the forest filling your belly and I'll be back with my friends. All we have to do is find a good place to cross the river."

Early the next morning they reach the roaring river. Logs from the timber camps rush past on their way to the sawmill.

It takes them all day to find a river crossing. Won Lin urges Toe Lai forward and quickly the elephant is neck-deep in the cool water. When they are halfway across, the rain lets up for a moment and the sun comes out from behind the clouds. On the other side of the river is the deep forest. They are almost home.

The authors would like to acknowledge the very kind assistance of His Excellency, Lieutenant General Chit Swe, Minister of Forestry, Union of Myanmar. We would also like to acknowledge the kind assistance of Myanmar Timber Enterprise and its superb staff, and the advice and expertise of the elephant veterinarians of Myanmar, who work so hard to take good care of the timber elephants. Finally, we are grateful for the support of our wives, Marie Smith and Anne M. Schmidt, who made this book possible by holding down the forts while we were in the forest with the elephants.